Joan

Miró

By Elizabeth Higdon

RIZZOLI ART SERIES

Series Editor: Norma Broude

Joan

Miró

(1893–1983)

THE ART of Joan Miró has long been admired for its considerable formal and technical merit. Recognized as among the most original of the painters sympathetic to Surrealism in the 1920s, Miró had an influence that was far-reaching and long lasting. Indeed the impact of his spontaneous techniques, organic abstraction, allover animation, and development of the color field on formalist abstract art can scarcely be overestimated.

As his stock among formalists went up over the years, so a tendency emerged to distance his efforts from those of the Surrealists, whose fascination with the theories of Sigmund Freud and Karl Marx, it was argued, overshadowed their interest in art as such. In 1948 the critic Clement Greenberg reasoned that Miró was never involved in Surrealism's "academic side," because "his grasp of what painting had to do in his time was too secure." According to Greenberg, Miró's ambition was principally formalist, based on the idea "of painting as an irrevocable two-dimensional medium" and on the belief that "modern painting can make effective statements only in accordance with this conception."[1]

As a consequence, any notion of political events or theories affecting Miró's art was peremptorily dismissed, and the artist was represented as utterly apolitical. "Among his friends," wrote curator James Soby in 1959, "Miró is known for his almost total lack of interest in political matters."[2] The sole exception was deemed to have been in the late 1930s, when "the fratricidal Spanish civil war forced him to take sides."[3]

While the formalist critics illumined Miró's well-deserved place among the great modernist innovators, they did so at a cost. Some of that was borne personally by the artist, who revealed late in life that the characterization of him as naive in matters outside art angered him and had even caused him some public humiliation.[4] More important to an understanding of his art was the omission by critics of whole realms of extra-artistic influence: the effects of time and place, background and aspirations upon even his most abstract art.

Ignored, too, was the matter of the censorship of Miró's art in Spain for nearly forty years: the Spanish government's unwillingness to recognize Miró from the end of the Spanish Civil War until the death of Generalissimo Francisco Franco in 1975. This matter is of no small importance to a discussion of meaning in Miró's art, for it tells us that his work was considered subversive and suspect by those authorities who, in the words of the artist himself, "always did everything possible so that I'd be unknown in my own country, while I was known everywhere else."[5] Very simply, the lack of attention to Miró and his art in Spain for so many years had to do with his being Catalan. Given the historical animosity between the province of Catalonia and the central government of Spain—dating back at least as far as the seventeenth century and also a factor in the civil war—Miró's identity and renown made him a special irritant to officials opposed to cultural practices reinforcing the existence of separate nations inside Spain. After the death of Franco, Miró was able to say, "I am not in favor of separatism. I am for Spanish unity, European unity, world unity."[6] Yet, the whole of his life, including his art, can be shown to have been deeply enmeshed in a Catalan struggle for freedom, for an autonomous expression that, while related to ideals of the modernist movement, had its immediate and experiential origins in his nation's fight for recognition and rights.

Placed side by side with events in Catalonia during his lifetime, Miró's art reveals an unswerving devotion to his people's highest aspirations: the freedom to speak their language, practice their customs, celebrate their myths, develop their industries and arts, and abide by their own laws without interference from Madrid. The modern Catalan autonomy movement is reflected both through the artist's drive toward technical and formal invention and, more particularly, through his development of a specific vocabulary of signs originating in a lexicon of patriotic emblems dear to the hearts of the Catalan liberationists.

This is not to say that Miró's art starts and stops with coded references to Catalan autonomy. Among its most consistently appealing qualities is the multivalency of its signs, the suggestion of constant metamorphosis. What the patriotic allusions afford is an extra dimension of meaning that deepens our appreciation for Miró's sources and motives and forever undermines the notion that his formalism necessarily excluded involvement in extra-artistic matters.

That Miró's art was affected by the Catalan autonomy movement was almost a matter of destiny. The painter was born in Barcelona, the ancient capital of Catalonia, in 1893, a few months after the signing of the Bases of Manresa, the document that transformed what had been a literary renaissance into a civic and political movement. When Miró was a year old, the Catalan politician Enric Prat de la Riba published the *Compendium of Catalanist Doctrine,* in which it was declared that Spain was not the fatherland, but was in fact Catalonia's "basic enemy."

The years of Miró's youth were marked by intense nationalist activity in which much attention was paid not only to political expressions of the need for autonomy, but also to the re-Catalanizing of everyday life. Even children participated. Miró's lifelong friend the poet J. V. Foix recalled, for example, that he and his schoolmates "prepared a handwritten newspaper . . . in which we talked about the language and asked that the school and all the books be in Catalan."[7] Miró, too, remembered that as a youth, "it was necessary to fight so that Catalan, our language, might be recognized as a cultural language."[8]

In 1910 the artist's parents purchased a *masia* (the traditional farmstead of Catalonia) southwest of Barcelona near Reus and the village of Montroig. Prompted no doubt by the movement's urging a reidentification with the soil of Catalonia and the ancient hearth and home, the Mirós acquired their *masia* precisely where the family had its roots

1. Apse decoration (lower register). Early twelfth century. Sant Pere de Burgal monastery church, Lérida, Spain. Museu Nacional d'Art de Catalunya, Barcelona. Photograph by Calveras/Sagristà

on the paternal side. It is this *masia* that would later be so lovingly celebrated, so carefully and exuberantly described in *The Farm* of 1921–1922 (plate 1). And it is the nearby town that would be proudly identified as Catalan, in effect politicized, by the national flag flying high above the houses in *Montroig, the Church and the Village* of 1919 (plate 2). Long viewed as evidence of the artist's personal devotion to nature and the rural life, works such as these may now be looked at afresh in the context of the times as expressions of the Catalans' romantic desire to find their soul in the farms and villages of their unique land.

It was during his first stay at the family farm that Miró decided on a career in art. In 1911 he enrolled at a design school in Barcelona run by the ardent Catalanist Francesc Galí, whose pedagogy reflected the orientation of the autonomy movement: toward the revival of Catalan traditions on the one hand, and toward integrating Catalonia into modern Europe on the other. Galí's purpose was to educate the nation's youth in their own Catalan culture—not as a variation of an alien and moribund Spanish tradition, but rather within the broader context of European humanism. Galí was also a great advocate of the popular "excursion," conceived then not as a mere field trip, but as a patriotic duty, a means of acquainting oneself with the land and its people. And he insisted that his students speak Catalan.[9]

One of the earliest of Miró's extant paintings, made in about 1914 while a student at Galí's, shows the figure of a man wearing the Catalan *barretina*, the traditional red "liberty cap." Despite the youthful clumsiness of the rendering, it is significant that Miró was already attempting the synthesis of old and new, traditional and modern prescribed by the movement. Taking as his subject the Catalan peasant, whose origins as a national symbol date back to the seventeenth-century revolt of *Els Segadors* (the Catalan Reapers), he updated its expression by adopting the exaggerated color and agitated brushwork of the Fauves.

The Catalan peasant symbol is alluded to again in Miró's *Self-Portrait* of 1919 (plate 3), in which, although he does not sport the *barretina*, he has donned the traditional crim-

son *garibaldina*. Besides noting the Cubist-inspired pattern of shadow and light on the artist's jacket, scholars have pointed repeatedly to the influence of the famed Catalan Romanesque frescoes, masterpieces of twelfth-century painting formerly located in churches throughout the province (fig. 1). Their impact is obvious in the intense frontal gaze of the figure, as well as in the schematic, linear, and decorative interpretation of hair, facial features, fabric folds, and surface patterning. What has been overlooked, however, is the context, the timeliness of the frescoes' influence and patriotic meaning.

Early in the century the promoters of Catalan autonomy focused on the need to identify and preserve Catalonia's cultural patrimony. Foremost among their efforts was the revival and renewal of the Catalan language, but there was also the cataloging and reproducing of the great medieval wall paintings. Likened in value to the national language, these murals were described as the Catalan's "national art."[10] After one of the murals was sold, it was decided that they would be removed from the province's churches and brought to Barcelona for display and safekeeping.

The murals were transferred and reinstalled between 1919 and 1924, just when their influence on Miró is clear. In addition to the self-portrait, other works of the period, such as *Montroig, the Church and the Village* and *The Farm*, also demonstrate the influence of the Romanesque style in their simplified shapes, linear emphases, and flattened areas of decorative patterning, all of which the artist related as well to Cubist geometry and dramatically foreshortened space. The significance of the older art is reinforced in Miró's view of Montroig by the prominence of the old village church, and in the self-portrait by the merging of peasant symbol and Romanesque sacred personage. By identifying himself in this very clear way with Catalonia's patriotic imagery and its cultural heritage, Miró acknowledged contemporary events and allied himself with the goals of autonomy.

In 1920 Miró went to Paris, then the nerve center of the art world, propelled there as much by the renewed vigor of artistic life after the First World War as by his own education and background, which had oriented him toward the modern and the cosmopolitan. During the early 1920s his style underwent a remarkable change, clearly affected by the art, old and new, that he encountered in the French capital. Registering, among other influences, his exposure to the work of the old-time fantasy painters Hieronymus Bosch and Pieter Bruegel and of newcomer Paul Klee, Miró embarked on a highly imaginative interpretation of nature, expressed via simplified graphic signs. Within one year he made the leap from the detailed, "naive" naturalism of *The Farm* to the startlingly spare abstraction of *The Hunter (Catalan Landscape)* (plate 6) and so to the forefront of the avant-garde.

But while Miró's style changed radically during his early years in Paris, his subjects, by and large, did not. Peasants and landscapes continued to dominate his art, and he used them to assert his Catalan identity. But he was creating something wholly new out of his Catalan roots. On a background painted in broad, flat bands of muted color resembling those found in the Romanesque murals, the peasant hunter in *The Hunter (Catalan Landscape)* is little more than a stick figure armed with a gun and a knife.[11] His ostensive prey is sprawled in the foreground, a curious, schematized combination of a rabbit and a fish, with the word fragment "sard" (from "sardine") beside it. To the hunter's left, a single leaf projects from a disk shape, the former intended to represent the carob tree, later described by the artist as a symbol for Catalonia.[12] The large disembodied eye attached to it recalls the eyes and the power of the gaze accentuated in the Romanesque frescoes. A ship at the far right displaying the Spanish flag is countered at upper left by a tiny airplane that bears the joined flags of Catalonia and France.

The suggestion that this painting "reads as an assertion of Catalan nationalism" deserves credit since the affiliation of signs here signals the artist's response to events occurring in his homeland.[13] By the end of the 1910s, intense social unrest in Barcelona had powerfully affected the Catalan movement, causing its petition to the Spanish parliament for autonomy to be shelved and creating a rift within the movement itself. Liberals in the movement identified with the internationalist spirit then animating both the labor movement and the emerging League of Nations. Evolving ever more rapidly toward separatism, they envisaged their future being within an international community of independent states. Instead, the outcome of the ongoing turmoil in Catalonia was Spain's submission in September of 1923 to the dictatorship of General Miguel Primo de Rivera. Among the new dictator's primary goals was the destruction of the Catalan autonomy movement, attempted first by placing a ban on the display of Catalan emblems and the official use of the Catalan language.

Miró's painting—with its abstracted (yet readable) allusions to his nation's emblems of resistance and vigilance, the Catalan peasant, the carob tree, the all-seeing eye, the Catalan flag (joined to the French flag in an obvious disassociation from the Spanish one)—thus acquired a striking political charge. In the context of current events in Catalonia, it must be concluded moreover that this image of an armed peasant is about more than the hunt. In fact the primary players in his apparently simple and whimsical scene may have been drawn for the same purposes of protest from two well-known Catalan folktales: one the story of the evil dragon (the fish-tailed rabbit as Primo?) slain by the brave Jordi (St. George, Catalonia's patron saint); the other that of the *mal caçador*, or accursed hunter, who is forever destined to hunt down the devil-as-rabbit.

Through subsequent years of dazzling formal invention and flirtation with the sparest forms of visual expression, Miró persisted in referring to the emblems of his homeland. In the series of four paintings from 1924–1925 titled *Head of a Catalan Peasant*, he reduced the subject's face to a simple cross scheme floating against a field of color. One version (plate 4) shows the peasant's red *barretina* atop the vertical axis of the cross emerging from a vast and brilliant yellow space, the juxtaposition of hues immediately calling to mind Catalonia's colors, crimson and yellow. The reduction of the facial features to eyes surrounded by radiating lines and to indications of a luxuriant beard recalls those features emphasized in the heads of apostles and saints in the Romanesque murals. In the upper right quadrant of the image is an abbreviated rainbow and a blue star.

This and other works of the period strike the viewer as most daring in their handling of color, each canvas presented as an expansive space of pure hue, organized and yet barely interrupted by the image configuration. No less bold, however, is the use of the emblem as a protest against the censorship of Primo de Rivera, who in 1924 dealt the cruelest blow of all by forcing the dissolution of the Catalans' governing body the Mancomunitat. Failing to obtain redress from the League of Nations, the left-wing Catalanists responded by recruiting broadly and becoming openly separatist. Heading the expanded movement now was the separatist party Estat Català centered in Paris. In its appeal to Catalans at home and abroad, Estat Català depended heavily on the plethora of banned Catalan emblems, including those associated with the revolt of the Segadors and the ill-fated war of independence of 1713–1714. The symbol of the party itself was the "solitary star, sign of liberty and indepedence," intended to be placed on a patch of blue and incorporated into the traditional Catalan flag once independence was achieved.[14] Miró's painting of the potent reminder of Catalan sovereignty at this particularly painful moment, his association of it with the sign of Catalan separatism (the star), and his use of the colors of the "new" Catalan flag, red, yellow, and blue, leave no doubt as to the artist's position respecting Catalan separatism.

Even in works of the period as seemingly divorced from visual reality as his great masterpiece *The Birth of the World* (plate 5), there are signs intimating Miró's preoccupation with his nation's plight and efforts toward its liberation. While the painting's background was created in a direct and spontaneous manner by splashing, rubbing, and dripping paint and glue onto the canvas, the few carefully painted foreground shapes were consciously conceived and arranged beforehand.[15] One of these "abstract" signs clearly resembles a great triangular black banner attached to a short post. In fact, in 1925 members of Estat Català had revived the *bandera negra* or black flag—the old emblem of the Segadors and later Catalan freedom fighters—with a vengeance, using it to designate the party's paramilitary sub-group, henceforth known as La Bandera Negra. Shortly before Miró began work on *The Birth of the World* at Montroig in the summer of 1925, members of La Bandera Negra made two much-publicized attempts on the life of the Spanish king.

Primo resigned in 1930. The following year, the parties of the Catalan left wing gained the elections and proclaimed an autonomous Catalan republic. Within months, Miró and his family left Paris and returned to Barcelona, to reside there more or less full time until the start of the Spanish Civil War in 1936.

The two years following his return were rich in variety and experimentation. Beginning in 1934, however, a newly aggressive and even angry tone entered Miró's art, which led to the use of the term *peintures sauvages* (wild paintings) to describe the works produced between that year and 1936 (plate 8). Gone was the lyrical charm and light-hearted humor of earlier days. The spaces of his pictures are occupied by monstrous figures, their limbs swollen and distorted, their garishly colored flesh modeled to appear bruised or infected, their mouths agape and teeth bared. His penchant for the comic darkened, becoming more fully allied to the grotesque. New tensions were registered too in his technique, which like the forms themselves is savagely animated. Typically interpreted as intimations of the coming wars, these *peintures sauvages* more likely disclose the artist's

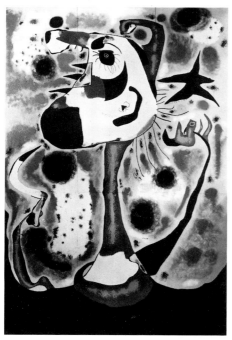

2. *The Reaper (Catalan Peasant in Revolt)*. 1937. Oil on Celotex, 18' ½" × 11' 11¾". Formerly in the pavilion of the Spanish Republic at the International Exposition, Paris. Now lost. Photograph courtesy Foundation Joan Miró, Barcelona

anguished response to the very present troubles threatening the demise of the Catalan republic.

The proof lies not merely in Miró's echoing the nerve-racking tensions and tragic stresses of the time in his forms and technique, but also in his choice of subject, which is again the Catalan peasant. Now the subject was more relevant than ever, as it pertained to the issue at the heart of Catalonia's present difficulties. In 1934 the Catalans had passed a law recognizing the rights of tenant farmers in disputes with landlords—an especially pressing issue in the midst of economic depression and widespread crop failure. But the Spanish government declared the law invalid. Thereafter, just at the time the distorted and ferocious figure of the Catalan peasant was at the center of Miró's art, so the rights of the Catalan tenant farmers were the focus of a fierce struggle between Madrid and the Catalan republic, with the Catalans viewing their support for agrarian reform as synonymous with a defense of their autonomy. As this struggle unfolded and the plight of the farmer worsened, the stage was set for the outbreak of civil war in July of 1936. Thus the anguish in Miró's art, as much as its grim humor, corresponds well with the events and mood just prior to the war, reflecting both the torment of the peasant farmers and the painful irony of the Catalan situation after so much elation and hope.

For the duration of the Spanish Civil War, Miró withdrew to Paris, where certain works he produced have long been interpreted as reactions to the conflict. In 1937 he reverted briefly to a naturalistic style in *Still Life with Old Shoe* (plate 9), responding thus not only to the gravity of events in Spain, but also to the popularity of Social Realism in much of the period's politically oriented art. As in *Farmers' Meal* from the period of the *peintures sauvages* (plate 8), the subject is the peasant repast, but now without peasants. Bereft of life other than that alluded to by the humble, abandoned objects themselves, the painting becomes an affecting symbol of suffering and loss, its hallucinatory color and ominous dark shadows contributing greatly to its unsettling effect.

Among the best known of Miró's works related to the civil war was the large mural, now lost, known as *The Reaper* (fig. 2), painted for the Spanish Pavilion at the International Exposition in Paris in 1937. Identified at the time as an image of the Catalan national anthem, "Els Segadors," the peasant is depicted in a warlike mode visually manifesting the refrain intoned by the "defenders of the land":[16]

A good sickle cut!
A good sickle cut,
If they want to take our wheat from us!
A good sickle cut!

Belligerency inhabited every part of Miró's *Reaper*, even his prominent *barretina* and upraised nose, both of which suggested the clenched fist salute of the Republicans' Popular Front. With his right hand, he brandished the traditional *falç* or sickle (according to legend, the Segadors attacked their Spanish oppressors with sickles and pitchforks), while his left hand strained toward the single star of Catalan independence. His torso rose out of the earth like a mighty tree, affirming his connection to the Catalan earth and recalling certain ancient depictions of the regenerative god Mithras.

By the time Franco's armies had defeated the Republicans in the spring of 1939, Miró's art had taken a decidedly different tack, devoid of the emotionalism of the preceding years, and so too, it seemed, of any connection to outside events. Entering into a period of intense stylistic refinement, Miró jettisoned extraneous detail (including indications of setting, modeling, and excess brushwork) and aimed at creating a style of immense internal harmony and external continuity. Largely immune to the influences of other artists' work of the day, he set about establishing the distinctive formal vocabulary that marked the rest of his career. The foundations were laid in several series, among them four paintings from July 1939 titled *The Flight of a Bird over the Plain* (plate 10) and twenty-three small works in gouache and oil known as the Constellations, which were begun in France in 1940 and completed in 1941 after the artist's return to Spain (see plate 11: *The Beautiful Bird Revealing the Unknown to a Pair of Lovers*).

With his attention once again fixed upon the simplified two-dimensional sign, Miró painted each colored shape in a single, unmodulated hue (changing color only where one flat form overlapped another) or outlined the form in black so that it became transparent to the color behind. Situating his signs upon a field of color that functioned as an expansive space of indeterminate depth and breadth, at first Miró allowed the signs to multiply, to become as dense as the star-studded sky alluded to in the Constellations. Even then the variety of such signs was limited by and large to flying creatures (usually birds), personages (male and female), celestial images (crescent moons and stars), eyes, sexual organ signs, and certain oft-repeated abstract shapes. Omnipresent in these works is a delicious sense of weightlessness, communicated by the signs floating in the color space and by a powerful aspirant movement, as figures and forms tend upward, assisted by upraised arms or wings suggesting both the ecstatic postures of figures in the Catalan Romanesque mural, and the postures of actual persons engaged in the Catalan national dance, the *sardana* (banned by Franco in the postwar period) (plates 11 and 12).

From this time forward, the generalized quality of Miró's signs would seem to preclude all associations or references beyond the playful and magical encounters among birds, persons, and stars indicated within the works themselves or conjured by their poetical titles. It may be argued, however, that while seeming to eschew the reality of the dictatorship in Spain with its absolute censorship of the Catalan movement, its taboos upon any sign of national identity, in fact Miró did not abandon his devotion to his homeland and the aspirations of its people. In the face of Franco's efforts to bury Catalan nationalism, Miró determined to make his art a substitute for the missing forms of national expression, to make it in effect speak Catalan where Catalan could not be spoken.

At the core of his restricted artistic vocabulary, the emblems of Catalonia persisted, albeit disguised or, better, transformed so that, while still in touch with their original forms and meanings, they offer to all, even the viewer unfamiliar with the "code," a heartening and vigorous message of liberation. Among such emblems, one may include the artist's palette dominated by the colors of Catalonia: the colors of the flag (crimson and yellow), plus blue (the color of Catalan separatism and the one most closely reflecting Catalonia's Mediterranean environment), green (for the evergreen carob tree, symbol of the nation's vitality) and, over the years, black (from the *bandera negra*).

Prominent in this connection too is the flying creature, always a bird who soars over the heads and upraised arms of Miró's personages, occasionally swooping down to mingle among them. The immediate visual association is with the multitude of winged creatures in the Catalan Romanesque murals. In a symbolic context however, the ever-present bird sign is more likely a reference to the popular patriotic poem chanted in defiance of Franco, "El Cant de la Senyera" ("The Song of the Flag"), in which the nation's flag is likened to a resplendent bird upon whom the eyes of all Catalans are fixed.

The banished symbol of the Catalan peasant remains central to Miró's art, where it is universalized as a sign for a man or a woman. That these figures relate to the peasant is supported by the presence of their traditional attributes, which themselves have acquired new guises and associations. The *barretina*, for example, is still present, as itself (that is, as a thumb-shaped cap either erect or deflated) or, more often, in the form of a large floppy nose or even as a free-floating phallic shape recalling the original meaning of the Phrygian bonnet as a sign of regeneration.

From earlier works, such as *Head of Catalan Peasant* and *The Reaper*, Miró distilled the star sign of "liberty and independence." Now persisting in either the five-pointed version or as an asterisk, the sign is everywhere. As important as the star are the peasant's tools, the traditional weapons of the Segadors, the sickle and the pitchfork. The latter takes on a multitude of associations, as it becomes a comb, an upraised hand, a crown, the tail feathers of a bird, and even a sign for the Catalan flag. In *Personage with Three Feet* (plate 13), a bronze of what was originally an assemblage of found objects, the upraised "arm" of the impish figure started out as an actual pitchfork, crude and hand-carved. In the final, cast version, the four-pronged fork has been painted bloody red in an unmistakable allusion to the four bright stripes of the Catalan flag.

3. *Volem l'Estatut* poster. 1977. Lithograph in color, 29½ × 21¼". Photograph courtesy Foundation Joan Miró, Barcelona

The all-important sickle appears over and over in the guise of the crescent moon. The formal relation between the moon and sickle is easy enough to see (for example in plates 11 and 12), as is the rhyming of the moon's shape with those of the figures' arms—the proximity of arms and moons reinforcing the meaning of the sign. That the association is more than a formal coincidence is driven home in the painting *Catalan Peasant in Moonlight* of 1968 (plate 14). There the peasant figure, itself a large curved shape in brilliant red and black against a green sky, rises up specterlike out of the massive blackness of the earth, his outstretched arm terminating in what is at once the peasant's tool/weapon and a glowing yellow moon. Not since *The Reaper* of 1937 had Miró so clearly identified the Segador as such, so frankly revealed his threatening aspect, only mildly dissembled through the poetry of the title.

In 1977 Miró was asked to design the official poster for the campaign aimed at obtaining a statute of autonomy for Catalonia (fig. 3). That he lived to see the success of that campaign was surely among the greatest rewards of his life. At his death, in 1983, the bulk of his work did not go to his heirs, but instead the artist chose "the voluntary gesture of offering my art to my country."[17] In fact, that gift had been given long before and renewed again and again over the years as, even from the splendid heights of international renown, Miró continued to identify his art with the aspirations of the Catalan people.

NOTES

(For short citations, refer to Further Reading)

1. Greenberg, *Miró*, p. 26
2. Soby, *Joan Miró*, p. 80.
3. Rubin, *Miró*, p. 72.
4. Raillard, *Ceci*, pp. 188–189.
5. Raillard, *Conversaciónes*, p. 233.
6. *Ibid.*, p. 238.
7. Albert Manent, "J. V. Foix te vuitanta anys: Entre la llegenda i la vida de cada dia," *Serra d'or* (Palma de Mallorca, Spain) 160 (January 1973), pp. 22–23.
8. Raillard, *Ceci*, p. 94.
9. *Ibid*, pp. 18–19, 94. Also, Alexandre Cirici, *L'Art català contemporani* (Barcelona: Edicions 62, 1969), p. 55 et passim.
10. J. Pijoan, *Les pintures murals catalanes*, 4 vols. (Barcelona: Institut d'Estudis Catalans, 1907–1921).
11. A chart identifying items in this painting was prepared by the curator William Rubin with the assistance of the artist. See Rubin, *Miró*, p. 22.
12. Raillard, *Conversaciónes*, pp. 230–231.
13. Gerta Moray, "Miró, Bosch and Fantasy Painting," *Burlington Magazine* 113, no. 820 (July 1971), p. 391.
14. Cucurell, *Panoràmica*, vol. 4, pp. 227–306.
15. It is at this point that Miró's work has been described as Surrealist, even though the artist himself was somewhat aloof from the movement. The description is based on the apparent similarity between his direct painting techniques and Surrealist automatism.
16. The identification of *The Reaper* with the Catalan national anthem was made by Juan Larrea, "Miroir d'Espagne, à propos du 'Faucheur' de Miró au pavillon espagnol de l'exposition 1937," *Cahiers d'art* 1, nos. 4–5, p. 15.
17. Raillard, *Ceci*, p. 163.

FURTHER READING

Cirici, Alexandre. *Miró Mirall*. Barcelona: Ediciones Polígrafa, S.A., 1977. English translation. *Miró and His World*. Barcelona: 1985.

Cucurell, Félix. *Panoràmica del nacionalisme català*. 4 vols. Paris: Editions Catalanes de Paris, 1975.

Dupin, Jacques. *Joan Miró: La Vie et l'oeuvre*. Paris, Flammarion, 1961. English translation. *Joan Miró: Life and Work*. New York: Harry N. Abrams, 1962.

Dupin, Jacques, et al. *Joan Miró: A Retrospective*. New York: Solomon R. Guggenheim Museum, 1987.

Greenberg, Clement. *Miró*. New York: Quadrangle Press, 1948. Reprint. New York: Arno Press, 1969.

Krauss, Rosalind, and Margit Rowell. *Joan Miró: Magnetic Fields*. New York: Solomon R. Guggenheim Foundation, 1972.

Miró, Joan. *Joan Miró, Carnets catalans*. Edited by Gaëtan Picon. Geneva: Editions d'Art Albert Skira, 1977. English translation. *Joan Miró, Catalan Notebooks*. New York: Rizzoli, 1977.

Penrose, Roland. *Miró*. London: Thames and Hudson, 1970. Reprint. New York: Thames and Hudson Inc., 1985.

Raillard, Georges. *Joan Miró, Ceci est la couleur de mes rêves: Entretiens avec Georges Raillard*. Paris: Editions du Seuil, 1977. Spanish translation, with one additional interview. *Conversaciónes con Miró*. Barcelona: Granica Editor, S.A., 1978.

Rowell, Margit, ed. *Joan Miró: Selected Writings and Interviews*. Boston: G. K. Hall and Co., 1986.

Rubin, William. *Miró in the Collection of the Museum of Modern Art*. New York: Museum of Modern Art, 1973.

Serra, Pere A. *Miró i Mallorca*. Barcelona, 1984. English translation, *Miró and Mallorca*. New York: Rizzoli, 1986.

Soby, James Thrall. *Joan Miró*. New York: Museum of Modern Art, 1959.

First published in 1993 in the United States of America by Rizzoli International Publications, Inc.
300 Park Avenue South
New York, New York 10010

Copyright ©1993 by Rizzoli International Publications, Inc.
Text copyright ©1993 by Elizabeth Higdon
All works by Miró ©1993 ARS, NY/ADAGP, Paris

Library of Congress Cataloging-in-Publication Data
Higdon, Elizabeth.
    Joan Miró/by Elizabeth Higdon.
    p. cm. — (Rizzoli art series)
    Includes bibliographical references and index
    ISBN 0-8478-1667-2
    1. Miró, Joan, 1893–1983—Criticism and interpretation.
    I. Title.
N7113.M54H54   1993
709'.2—dc20   92–41496
                                                      CIP

Series Editor: Norma Broude

Series designed by José Conde and Betty Lew/Rizzoli
Editor: Charles Miers; Assistant Editor: Jennifer Condon

Printed in Italy

Front cover: See colorplate 14

Index to Colorplates

1. *The Farm*. 1921–1922. In this early masterpiece, Miró perfected his "naive" realism, compiling in amusing and obsessive detail a visual catalogue of the family *masia*, including the farmhouse and related structures as well as the flora and fauna. Influenced by native Catalan art, Miró also reveals a modernist flattening of form and crisp rendering of geometric patterns.

2. *Montroig, the Church and the Village*. 1919. Here the artist offers an extremely accurate depiction of the old village, while also registering the animated linearity of traditional Romanesque painting and of contemporary styles. The Catalan identity of the locale is stressed through the presence of the national flag, the prominent medieval church, and the peasant in traditional costume.

3. *Self-Portrait*. 1919. The young Miró is dressed in the short red jacket of the Catalan peasant, a symbol of Catalan nationalism dating back to 1640. The strict frontality of the image and its severe expression are borrowed from the sacred figures in the famed Catalan Romanesque murals. In its dual identification, the self-portrait becomes a powerful expression of the artist's patriotism.

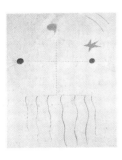

4. *Head of a Catalan Peasant*. 1924. Situated within a field of color, the peasant's face has been reduced to a simple cross scheme with disks for eyes and undulating lines to indicate a beard. The attributes of the national symbol have been pared to the red *barretina* (the traditional "liberty cap"), which is meaningfully associated here with the blue star and the colors of free Catalonia.

5. *Birth of the World*. 1925. Viewed as a rare instance of Miró's pure abstraction, this is also considered an example of Surrealist-inspired automatism, a process of free-association. In fact, the spontaneity was limited to the background field, with the foreground abstracted shapes consciously conceived. The black banner here, a likely allusion to Catalan separatism, contradicts the notion of pure abstraction.

6. *The Hunter (Catalan Landscape)*. 1923–1924. After his move to Paris in 1920, Miró's art underwent a radical transformation, seen in the use of abbreviated, graphic signs. Here the cryptic references to the emblems of Catalonia—the peasant, the all-seeing eye, the carob tree, the Catalan flag—belie the painting's innocent surface, revealing the artist's opposition to the Spanish dictator Primo de Rivera.

7. *Landscape (The Grasshopper)*. 1926. In this simple and whimsical interpretation of nature, including an amoeba-like grasshopper at upper right, the inscription of the artist's name across the terrain reinforces his identification with Catalonia, while the flags of several nations flying from the ship's mast suggest his subscription to the popular idea of a free Catalonia within a family of independent states.

8. *Farmers' Meal*. 1935. From the body of Miró's works known as the *peintures sauvages*, or wild paintings, on account of their unprecedented emotionalism in both form and techniques, this painting updates the traditional "merry company" theme of peasants at table, conveying a dark mood and savage humor through grotesquely animated figures and farmyard creatures.

9. *Still Life with Old Shoe*. 1937. In an anomalous reversion to a naturalistic style, Miró reflects the impact of Social Realism on politically oriented art of the time, endowing the humble objects of peasant life with a hallucinatory presence by contrasting bright, unreal color with ominous dark shadows.

10. *The Flight of a Bird over the Plain III*. 1939. At this point in his career, Miró refocused his art on the two-dimensional sign within a vast color field. The prominence of the bird in this series sets a precedent for later works and may hark back to the multitude of winged creatures in the Catalan Romanesque murals.

11. *The Beautiful Bird Revealing the Unknown to a Pair of Lovers*. 1941. In the Constellations series, Miró created dense weblike configurations out of the birds, stars, moons, and personages from his newly established vocabulary of signs, allowing the allover animation of form to suggest the star-studded sky after which the series was named.

12. *Women in the Night*. 1946. As in Miró's many works from 1940 on where appealing formal harmonies and childlike renderings only partly conceal the artist's response to postwar censorship in Spain, here the figures' postures echo those of real persons engaged in the Catalan national dance, the sardana, while the repetition of the sickle shape suggests the symbol of Catalan resistance.

13. *Personage with Three Feet*. 1967. In this assemblage of found objects later cast in bronze, a puckish three-legged figure raises aloft what was once a crude pitchfork. Besides its amusing metamorphosis into a four-fingered hand, the bright red fork evokes the old weapon of the Segadors as well as the four crimson stripes of the Catalan flag.

14. *Catalan Peasant in Moonlight*. 1968. In this, Miró's most emphatic allusion to the Segadors since the Spanish Civil War, the simple curved shape of the peasant in glowing red and black rises ominously from the dark plane of the earth. The merging of sickle and crescent moon here tends to support the meaning of the recurrent crescent shape in Miró's art as a sign of Catalan resistance.

15. *Birds at the Birth of Day*. 1970. The extroversion of Miró's later years is evidenced in this painting's scale and execution. Splashes of black paint and bold calligraphic marks interspersed with patches of color reflect the vitality of the aging artist as well as the angry protest and energetic optimism of the times.

1. *The Farm.* 1921–1922. Oil on canvas, 48¼ × 55⅝".
©1992 National Gallery of Art, Washington, D.C., Gift of Mary Hemingway

2. *Montroig, the Church and the Village.* 1919. Oil on canvas, 28¾ × 24".
Private collection. Photograph courtesy Foundation Joan Miró, Barcelona

3. *Self-Portrait.* 1919. Oil on canvas, 28¾ × 25⅝".
Musée Picasso, Paris. Giraudon/Art Resource, New York

4. *Head of a Catalan Peasant.* 1924. Oil on canvas, 57½ × 45".
©1992 National Gallery of Art, Washington, D.C. Gift of the Collectors Committee

5. *The Birth of the World.* 1925. Oil on canvas, 98¾″ × 78¾″. The Museum of Modern Art, New York.
Acquired through an anonymous fund, the Mr. and Mrs. Joseph Slifka and Armand G. Erpf Funds, and by gift of the artist.
Photograph ©1992 The Museum of Modern Art, New York

6. *The Hunter (Catalan Landscape)*. 1923–1924. Oil on canvas, 25½ × 39½".

7. *Landscape (The Grasshopper)*. 1926. Oil on canvas, 44⅞ × 57½".

8. Farmers' Meal. 1935. Oil on cardboard, 29½ × 41¾".
Private collection

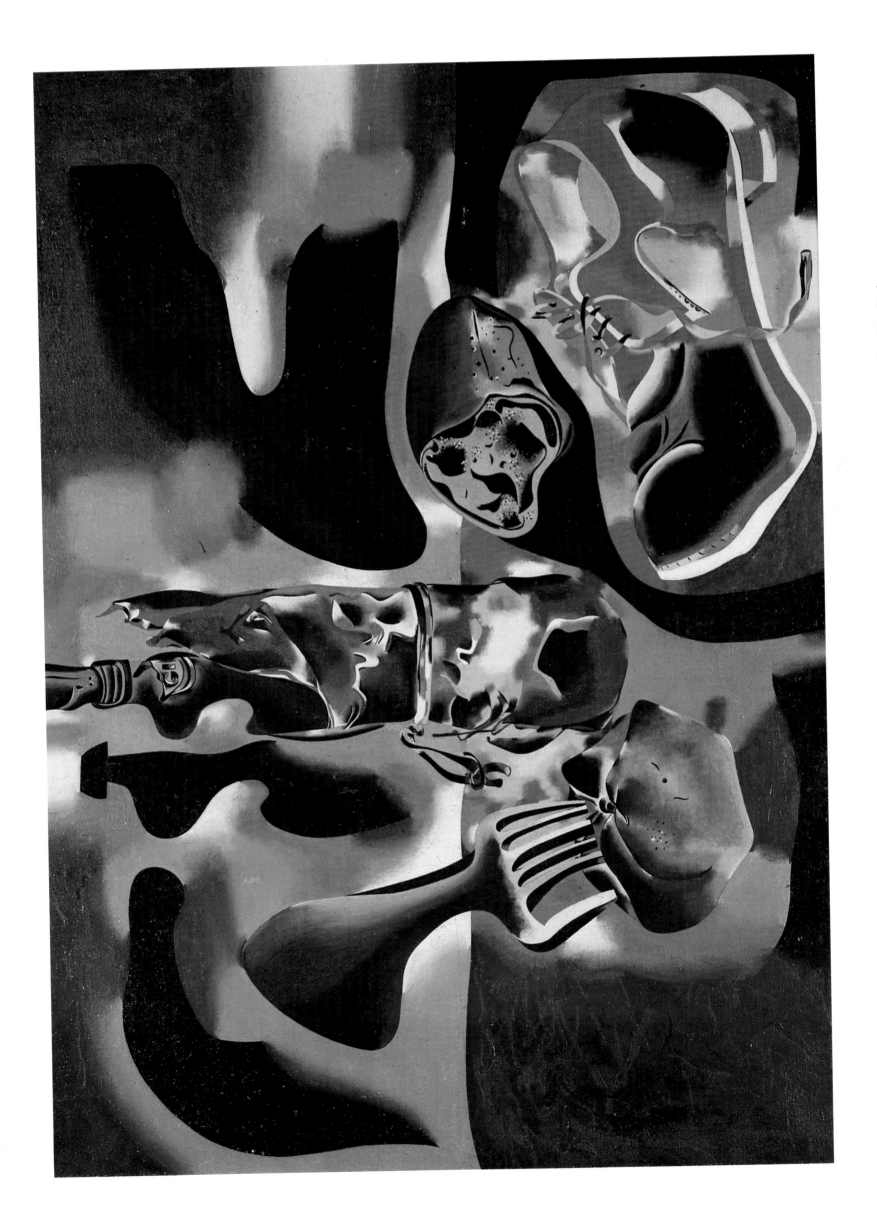

9. *Still Life with Old Shoe.* January 24–May 29, 1937. Oil on canvas, 32 × 46″. The Museum of Modern Art, New York. Gift of James Thrall Soby. Photograph ©1992 The Museum of Modern Art, New York

10. *The Flight of a Bird over the Plain III.* July 1939. Oil on burlap, 35¼ × 45½". Solomon R. Guggenheim Museum, New York. Gift, Evelyn Sharp, 1977. Photograph by David Heald ©The Solomon R. Guggenheim Foundation, New York

11. *The Beautiful Bird Revealing the Unknown to a Pair of Lovers.* 1941. Gouache and oil wash on paper, 18 × 15".
The Museum of Modern Art, New York. Acquired through the Lillie P. Bliss Bequest.
Photograph ©1993 The Museum of Modern Art, New York

12. *Women in the Night.* 1946. Oil on canvas, 14 × 12".
Private collection, New York

13. *Personage with Three Feet.* 1967. Painted bronze, height: 85½".
Foundation Joan Miró, Barcelona

14. *Catalan Peasant in Moonlight.* 1968. Acrylic on canvas, 63⅜ × 51⅛".
Foundation Joan Miró, Barcelona

15. *Birds at the Birth of Day*. 1970. Oil on canvas, 86⅝ × 102¾".